For satisfaction
every time ... chocolate!

Susan & Terry
Chocolate Moose
April 1996

D0579614

CHOCOLATE

Sex

A NAUGHTY LITTLE BOOK

BY

A. Richard Barber & Nancy R.M. Whitin

With photographs by Anthony Loew

WARNER BOOKS

A TIME WARNER COMPANY

Warner Books, Inc., 1271 Avenue of the Americas, New York, NY 10020

 A Time Warner Company

Printed in the United States of America

First Printing: November 1994

10 9 8 7 6 5 4 3 2 1

Library of Congress Cataloging-in-Publication Data

Barber, A. Richard , 1940–
    Chocolate sex : a naughty little book / A. Richard
Barber & Nancy R.M. Whitin; with photographs by
Anthony Loew.
    p.   cm.
ISBN: 0-446-51812-3
    1. Chocolate—humor. 2. Sex—humor. I. Whitin,
Nancy R.M. II. Loew, Anthony. III. Title.
PN6231.C33B37   1994
818' .5402—dc20   94-9623
                                                   CIP

DESIGN AND PRODUCTION PROVIDED BY ROBERT BULL DESIGN

CHOCOLATE
Sex

"Women are ethereal beings, subsisting entirely on chocolate . . . ."

— OGDEN NASH

CHOCOLATE SEX

AN INTRODUCTION

*W*HAT IS IT THAT WOMEN REALLY CRAVE: above jewelry, above clothes, even above shoes? Dare we say it — even above men? It is chocolate. Yes, chocolate — chocolate, and more chocolate. The smell of chocolate. Its velvet brown color. Its taste. Most of all, there is no greater sensation for women than the consumption of chocolate. Bliss overtakes a woman as the musky sweetness caresses the inside of her mouth, lingers on her tongue, and sends her tastebuds reeling. Long after the last morsel of chocolate is consumed, the memories remain . . . are they lustful sighs, or heart-pounding flashbacks?

Women lust after chocolate. Their desire for it is overpowering; no matter how hard a woman tries to restrain herself with visions of tight black dresses or tiny bikinis, she knows in her heart she will ultimately succumb to chocolate's seductive call.

Why, you might ask, are men blind to the carnal power of chocolate? Why, oh why, do they waste their time on flowers? No floral scent can measure up to the aphrodisial aroma of pure, unadulterated chocolate. Why spend money on diamonds? You can't lick diamonds off your fingers! Why, why, why do men buy women fur coats? Fur may warm the body, but the soul is left naked and untouched. A Mercedes?!? Forget it! Fill the trunk with truffles and a woman will consider it. What good is anything else? There is nothing, nothing but chocolate!

Scientists have found that substances in chocolate combine with the body's natural chemical makeup to raise one's blood pressure, heart rate and glucose levels, resulting in a sensation that can be likened to only one other feeling: orgasm.

To hell with science! As far as women are concerned, chocolate is ecstasy. End of story.

It is indeed the sly and scheming man who knows and uses the power of chocolate. It is the man with superior ego strength who can take second place to a two-pound box of hand-dipped chocolate cherries — it is that man who will be known as a bon vivant, a seducer, a soulmate, a devastating sensualist, a hedonist, a truly irresistible lover.

In fact, it doesn't matter how handsome a man is, or how he's built, or how thick his wallet, or whether his car is sleek, or even whether his position is powerful. Because the only thing that really matters is that he understands a woman's real needs. And women need . . . chocolate.

first cho

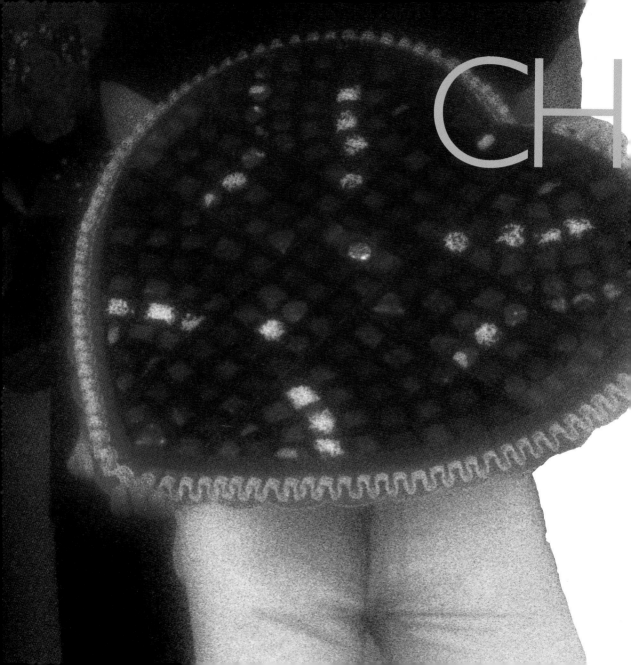

OCOLATE
foreplay

THE CHOCOLATE INDEX

Amount spent on chocolate for Valentine's Day last year: $580,425,000

Amount of chocolate sold in the U.S. last year: 5,659,410,000 pounds

Percentage of women who think about chocolate while having sex: 86%

Percentage of men who have ever thought about chocolate when having sex: 1%

Percentage of women who think about sex when eating chocolate: 98%

Percentage of women who think eating chocolate is sex: 78%

Maximum number of orgasms achieved by a woman during sex as documented by Masters and Johnson: 19

Maximum number of orgasms achieved by a woman eating chocolate: 43

Number of calories burned during a passionate kiss: 26

Number of calories in a Hershey's Chocolate Kiss: 25

Adorable chocolate

white
chocolate

milk chocolate

bittersweet

What woman can think of men
so long as she has
an endless supply of chocolate?

chocolate

chocolate
innocence

"A piece of . . . chocolate, Mrs. Robinson?"

Sex, Lies, and . . .

Freud and C

HOCOLATE

Chocolate

guilt

TOP TEN REASONS TO EAT
CHOCOLATE

10. The ice cream just didn't seem to be working by itself.
9. Haven't had any in over 30 minutes.
8. Haven't had anything else in over 30 days.
7. Didn't meet budget again this month. Sales down 20%.
6. No other choice, I would have starved to death otherwise.
5. It's Saturday night and I just finished doing the laundry.
4. Had a desire to do something very naughty that I'd later regret.
3. Eleven days late and I've checked the calender 6 times today.
2. Tried on 27 swim suits.
1. PMS

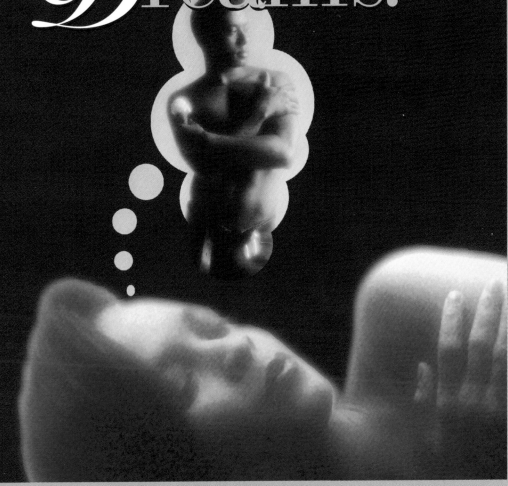

A Chocolate Fantasy

I AM WALKING ALONG THE BEACH at the north end of Malibu. A handsome young man riding bareback on a sorrel horse with a golden mane, and his chocolate Labrador are romping toward me. The dog runs ahead of his master and drops a stick of driftwood at my feet. He bounces up and down with delight. His red bandana scarf flaps in the ocean breeze. I am enchanted and toss the stick into the surf for him. His master dismounts. He is tan, gold streaks in his hair... what a smile, what a body! He apologizes if his dog, "D.C.," was bothering me, but he can't keep him away from beautiful women. I am more than enchanted! His accent sounds European. I ask what "D.C." stands for. He answers, "Deep Chocolate, of course." We ride together back to his beachhouse. He opens a bottle of champagne and a box of truffles. We sit on his deck sipping the wine and nibbling the truffles as the sun begins to sink behind his sailboat bobbing against the dock. Deep Chocolate lies patiently at our feet. Just as the sun disappears in a marvelous flash of light, he whispers in my ear, "My father owns a Belgian chocolate company . . ."

Chocolate
dependency

chocolate enabler

Powerful as the pounding surf are the chocolate passions of woman, all different, and all, base and noble alike, are first under her control, and afterward used by cruel men to dominate her.

Chocolate

Lust

SIMULTANE
CHOCOL

chocolate
cheesecake

Where's the man
could ease a heart
like chocolate?

the perfect lover

At 3:00 A.M. he turns into a box of chocolate truffles and a bottle of ice cold

champagne.

So sweet . . .

and
Sticky

chocolate
decadence

Bon Bon Mots

- We divide all chocoholics into two classes: those who eat chocolate to remember and those who eat chocolate to forget.

- When we get a little money, we buy chocolates; and if any is left, we buy food and clothes.

- If a woman makes a fool of herself over chocolate does that make the things she behaves sensibly about any less real or true or important?

- When we encounter another woman of rare intellect, we ask her what kind of chocolate she likes.

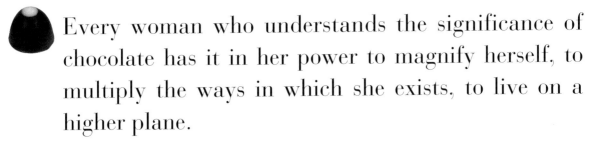 Every woman who understands the significance of chocolate has it in her power to magnify herself, to multiply the ways in which she exists, to live on a higher plane.

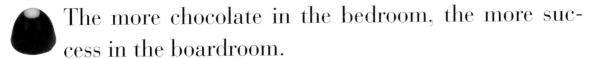 Madness is chocolate put to good use.

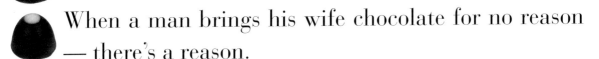 The more chocolate in the bedroom, the more success in the boardroom.

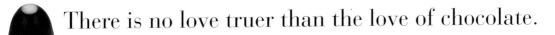 There is no love truer than the love of chocolate.

 When a man brings his wife chocolate for no reason — there's a reason.

Without chocolate, life would be long.

Old age means realizing you will never have all the chocolate you wanted.

.chocolate
interruptus

CHOCO
Pervers

OLATE
ions

rocky road

bondage

ral

chocolate

"Ello. You have reach Monsieur Chip, your personal chocolate lover. You need chocolate, no?"

"Oh, yes. Please, please talk semi-sweet to me now."

"I only do desserts."

"Yes, desserts. Let's get to the desserts. Hurry, I really need it."

"But of course. Right now I am looking at ze brownie . . . à la mode."

"Muh, more. I can't stand it. Go quicker."

"Zere is hot fudge oozing all over it."

DIAL 1-900-CHO

"Oh, no... tell me about the fudge sauce . . . hurry!"

"Oui. It is warm, very warm, gooey and sticky, tres sticky . . . chocolate . . . Mon Dieu . . . You wish to know what Monsieur Chip look like?"

"What? NO! Is the brownie homemade?"

"Oui, oui! Can you not see it? It is very, very thick. It has nuts. I am biting into it now. M-m-m-m . . ."

"Oh . . . oh. How does it feel? What are you doing with it now?"

"I am roll ze brownie around inside my mouth. Zere is whipped cream all over my lips. I am lick ze fudge sauce off my fingers . . . Un, deux... trois. M-m-m-m-m-m!"

"Oh, God . . . God, it's prem-ma-a-a-a-ture chocolate!"

"Ah, mais oui, bon . . . bon. You want know what really turn on Monsieur Chip?"

"No. Yes . . . What? What?"

"Eating ze devil's food cake hot from ze oven. Ze buttercream frosting is still warm in ze bowl. I am eating zem both simultaneously. Oops! Look at zat. I have drop ze à la mode in my, how you say . . . lap, lap. You wish to help me clean up?"

"Moi ? ? ?"

The Last

Temptation

ACKNOWLEDGMENTS

In the spirit of chocolate fellowship there are a number of people we must acknowledge and thank:

The beach scene that accompanies our "Chocolate Fantasy" is reproduced with the permission of FPG International.

The sensuous photograph of the Chocolate Pear Dessert that illustrates "Chocolate Lust" was taken by Katrina DeLeon and is reproduced with the permission of Still Life Stock, Inc.

"Adam and Eve" is from a 1504 engraving by Albrecht Durer.

The painting of "The Last Supper" by Leonard da Vinci's student, Marco da Oggiono, is reprinted by permission of Art Resource.

James Cagney's infamous still is from *Public Enemy*, a 1939 Warner Bros. film.

Many of the boxes of hand-dipped chocolates were provided coutesy of Martha Bond of Li-Lac Chocolates in New York City. The wondrous solid chocolate leg of "Mrs. Robinson" and other cast chocolates were courtesy of John Whaley of Fifth Avenue Chocolatier, located on Madison Avenue.

And last, and never least, we must thank our editor, Liv Blumer, her assistant, Caryn Karmatz, and our designer, Bob Bull. Their enthusiasm, support, and love of chocolate often surpassed our own.

Fellow Chocoholics:
During the writing, photography, and production of Chocolate Sex, we discovered a great many people were eager to reveal their own secret "Chocolate Sexual Fantasies and Dreams." We invite you to participate as well. Please send us your own creative chocolate fantasies for possible inclusion in our next book.
Send to:

Chocolate Fantasies
P.O. Box 887
Kent, CT 06757